For the A in my alphabet

Pushkin Press
71–75 Shelton Street
London WC2H 9JQ

Text and illustrations copyright © 2022 by Ellen Heck

A is for Bee was first published in the USA by Levine Querido, 2022

First published by Pushkin Press in 2022

1 3 5 7 9 8 6 4 2

ISBN 13: 978-1-78269-362-8

Book design by Jon Gray, Ellen Heck, and Semadar Megged.
The text type was set in Caslon. Hand lettering by Jon Gray.
The art for this book was created on scratchboard.
The panels were scanned and enlarged to show texture,
then digitally coloured and arranged.

Printed and bound in China by C&C Offset Printing Co., Ltd.

www.pushkinpress.com

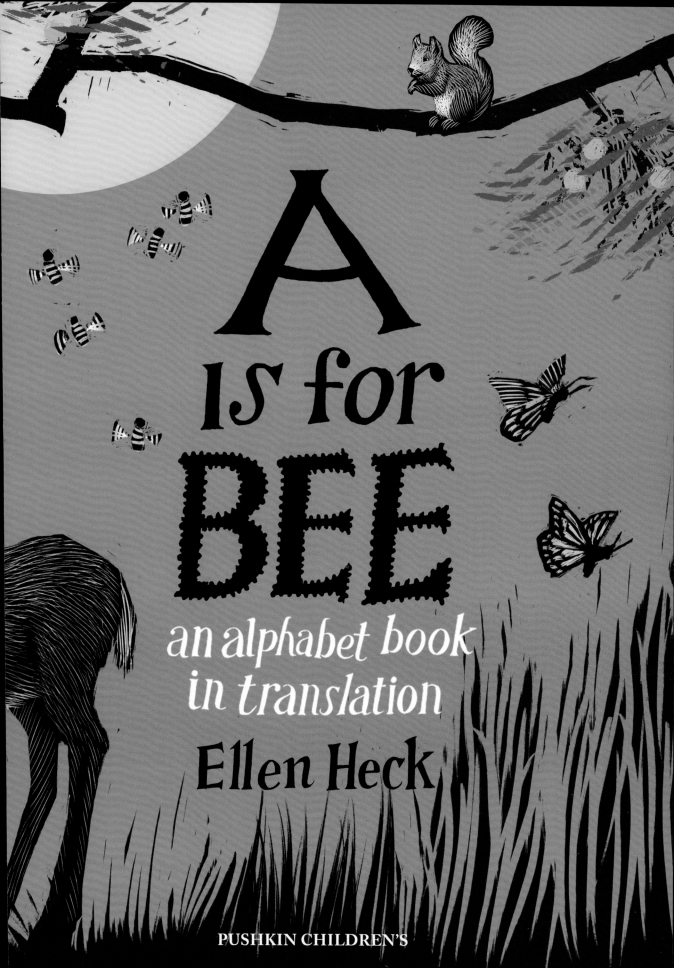

A is for BEE

an alphabet book
in translation

Ellen Heck

PUSHKIN CHILDREN'S

We speak to each other in many languages,
and in some of them . . .

A is for BEE

Anụ̄
in Igbo

Arı
in
Turkish

Aamoo
in
Ojibwe

Abelha
in
Portuguese

Biri
in
Hausa

Bojog
in
Balinese

Beždžionė
in
Lithuanian

Bandar
in
Hindi

B is for **Monkey**

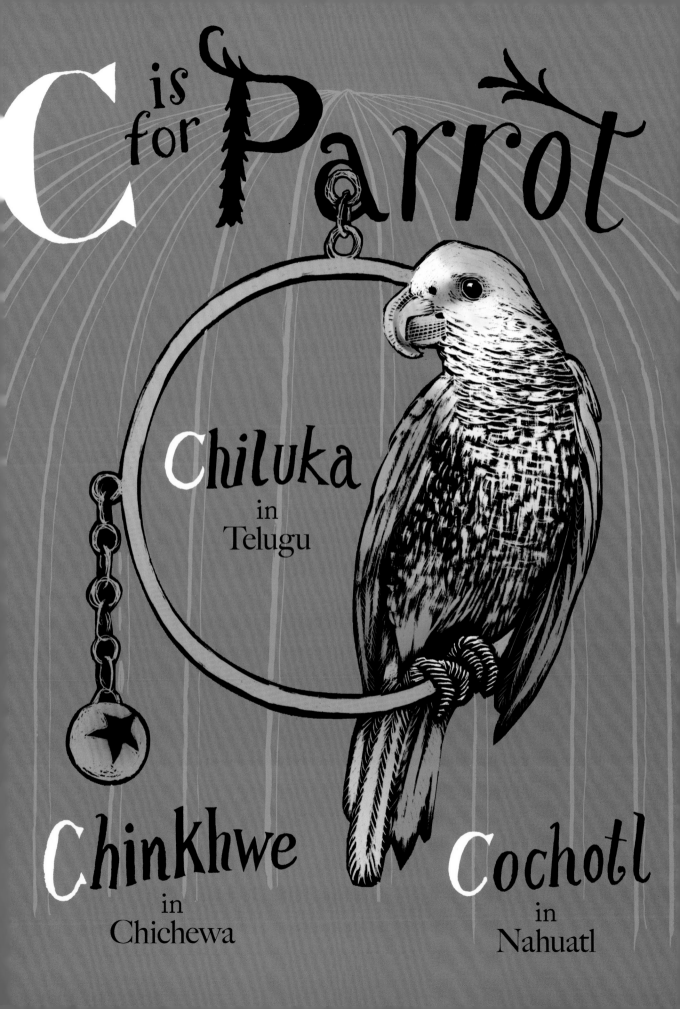

C is for Parrot

Chiluka
in Telugu

Chinkhwe
in Chichewa

Cochotl
in Nahuatl

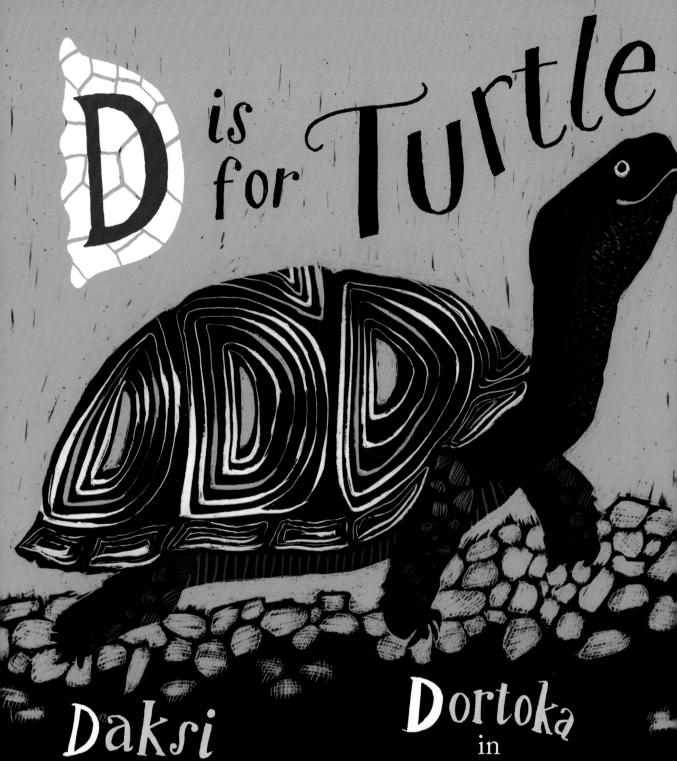

D is for Turtle

Daksi
in
Cherokee

Dortoka
in
Basque

Deckelsmouk
in
Luxembourgish

Dtào
in
Thai

Etmaewig
in Chechen

Escargot
in French

Etana
in Finnish

E is for Snail

Elagwa
in Cherokee

Gato
in
Spanish

Gaazhagens
in
Ojibwe

Goyangi
in
Korean

G is for Cat

H is for tiger

Huli
in
Kannada

Harimau
in
Indonesian

Inhlanzi
in Zulu

Ikan
in Malay

Iqalluk
in Alutiiq

I is for fish

Iwak
in Javanese

Isda
in Tagalog

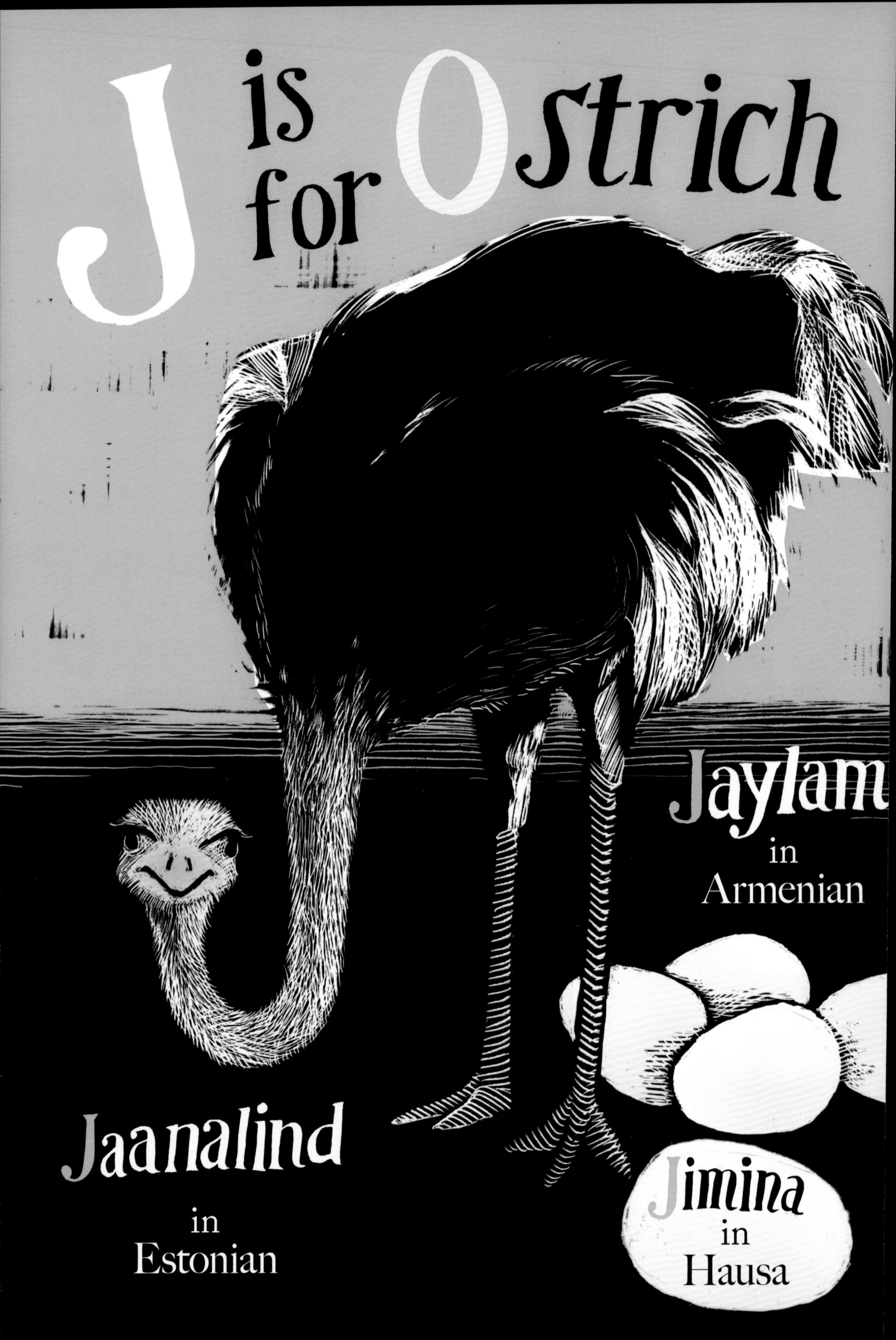

J is for Ostrich

Jaylam
in
Armenian

Jaanalind
in
Estonian

Jimina
in
Hausa

Kakīroa in Māori

K is for giraffe

Kirahvi in Finnish

Kaelkirjak in Estonian

Kamilopárdali in Greek

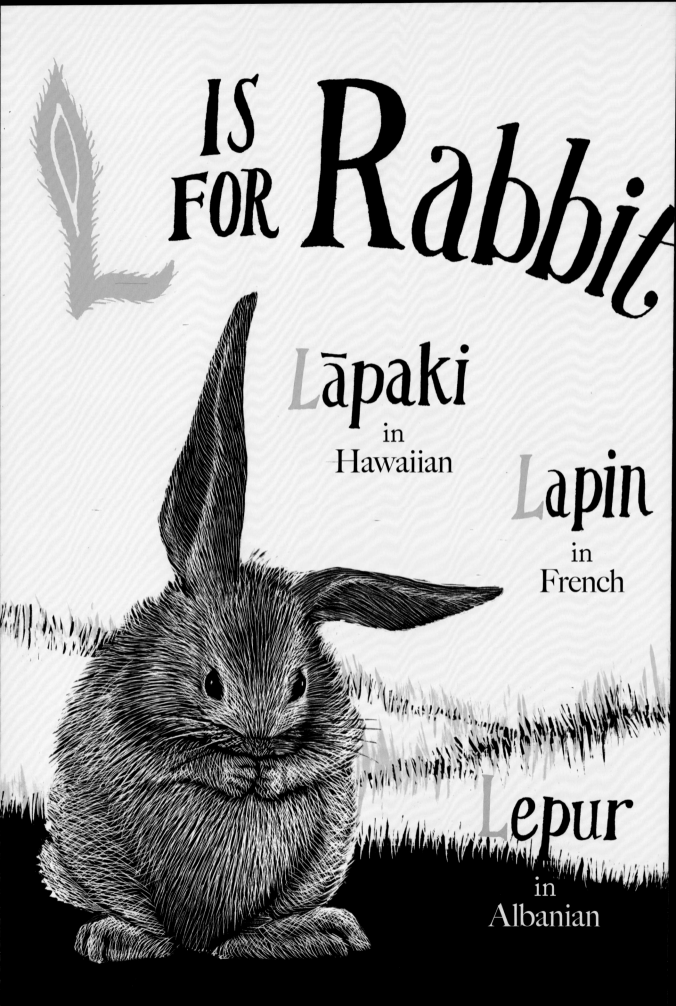

L IS FOR Rabbit

Lāpaki
in Hawaiian

Lapin
in French

Lepur
in Albanian

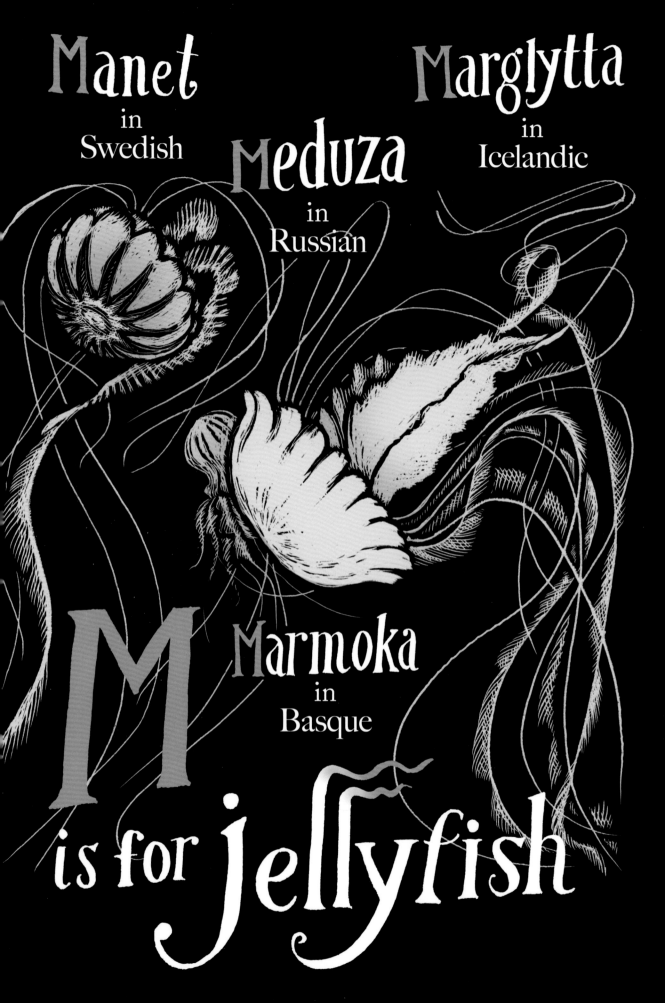

Manet
in Swedish

Marglytta
in Icelandic

Meduza
in Russian

Marmoka
in Basque

M is for jellyfish

N IS FOR Sloth

Namuneulbo
in Korean

Ndilna'i
in Navajo

Namakemono
in Japanese

Odler
in Yiddish

Orzeł
in Polish

Orel
in Ukrainian

O is for Eagle

Plameňák
in
Czech

Pariwana
in
Quechua

Parina
in
Aymara

P IS FOR flamingo

Q is for frog

Qīngwā
in
Mandarin

Qurbağa
in
Azerbaijani

R IS FOR fox

Ræv
in
Danish

Rovî
in
Kurdish

Renard
in
French

Róka
in
Hungarian

Rubâh
in
Persian

T is for Octopus

Tako
in
Japanese

Tmanun
in
Hebrew

Tintenfisch
in
German

Undar
in
Gujarati

Ukucha
in
Quechua

Undīr
in
Marathi

U is for Mouse

V is for Zebra

Varikkutirai in Tamil

Wahid Alqarn
in
Arabic

Wānga-lànga
in
Wolof

Wiyil
in
Somali

W is for rhinoceros

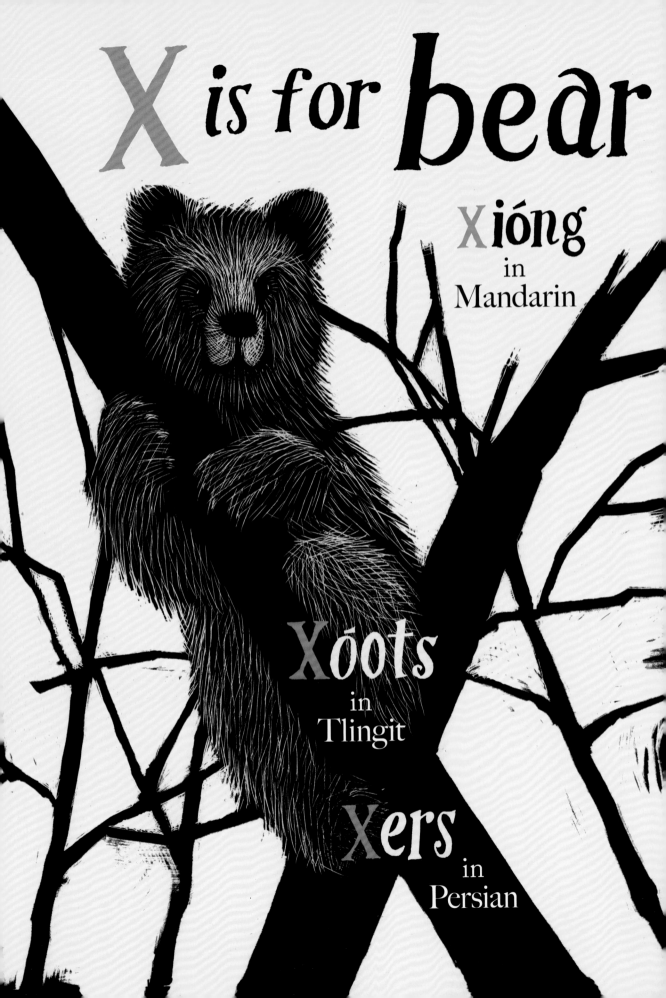

X is for bear

Xióng
in Mandarin

Xóots
in Tlingit

Xers
in Persian

Y is for porcupine

Yamaarashi
in
Japanese

Ystervark
in
Afrikaans

Z is for elephant

z**aan**
in
Mongolian

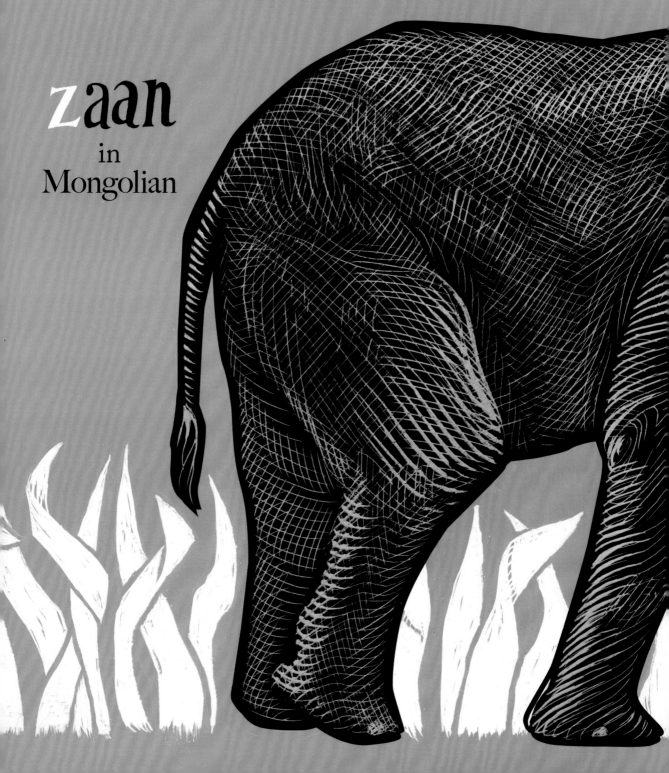

zehon
in
Amharic

zilonis
in
Latvian

zō
in
Japanese

To listen to native or fluent speakers
pronouncing words
that appear in this book,
please scan the QR code below

Words from the languages represented in this book can be found on these alphabet pages:

Afrikaans	Y	Hebrew	T	Navajo	N
Albanian	F, L	Hindi	B, S	Ojibwe	A, G
Alutiiq	I	Hungarian	R	Persian	R, X
Amharic	Z	Icelandic	M	Polish	O
Arabic	F, W	Igbo	A	Portuguese	A
Armenian	J	Indonesian	H	Quechua	P, U
Aymara	P	Irish	F	Russian	M
Azerbaijani	Q	Italian	F	Somali	W
Balinese	B	Japanese	N, T, Y, Z	Spanish	G
Basque	D, M	Javanese	I	Swahili	S
Chechen	E	Kannada	H	Swedish	M
Cherokee	D, E	Korean	G, N	Tagalog	I
Chichewa	C	Kurdish	R	Tamil	V
Czech	P	Latvian	Z	Telugu	C
Danish	R	Lithuanian	B	Thai	D, S
Estonian	J, K	Luxembourgish	D	Tlingit	X
Finnish	E, K	Malay	I	Turkish	A
French	E, L, R	Malayalam	S	Ukrainian	O
German	T	Mandarin	Q, X	Vietnamese	S
Greek	K	Māori	K	Wolof	W
Gujarati	U	Marathi	U	Yiddish	O
Hausa	B, J	Mongolian	Z	Zulu	I
Hawaiian	L	Nahuatl	C		

Author's Note

The words and languages in this book have been chosen for a variety of reasons, each of which has brought to light something I didn't know at the start of the project.

The featured animals are those that readers have probably seen before in alphabet books. Imagining translations of many different abecedaries all in one place, I tried to arrange familiar animals in an order that would be noticeably new. For example, in English, we are used to seeing *Z is for Zebra* on the final page. Rearranging the animals so that each would be represented by a handful of different-sounding translations that all begin with roughly the same sound or letter was a big puzzle and a lot of fun. In several languages, the spelling of a noun changes depending on whether it is definite or indefinite. In other languages, the commonly used English animal names were too general for direct translation. For example, in Tlingit, a language indigenous to the northwest coast of North America, where brown bears (*Ursus arctos*) and black bears (*Ursus americanus*) live, these two different species are not commonly grouped together but instead distinguished as *xóots* (brown bear) and *s'eek* (black bear). Similarly, in Nahuatl, a language spoken in Mexico and Central America, there is not a general word for all types of parrots, so *cochotl* refers to one of the most common in the area, the white-fronted parrot (*Amazona albifrons*). I've tried to reflect this in the illustrations.

When writing words in English, we use the Roman alphabet, which is also called the Latin alphabet. It represents different sounds with letters. Lots of languages use a version of the Roman alphabet. Because of this, if you can read in English you are able to sound out words in those other languages, such as Italian or Spanish. You may not know the meaning of the words you are reading, but you are still able to *say* them. However, many languages use their own unique writing systems. So, for English readers to be able to say words from these languages, the words must be *transliterated*. To transliterate is to take a word from a language with its own sounds and writing system and use the closest corresponding symbols or letters to write that word in a different writing system. This way, someone who does not know the language is still able to make the *sounds* of that word in that language. And of course, this is not always a simple task. For example, in Thai, the word for *turtle* is เต่า. At first, I did not know which sounds to make to say that word because I cannot speak or read Thai. So, I looked up the transliteration—in this case, the *Romanization*, which is transliteration from one language into the Roman alphabet. It turns out there are two different Romanizations of Thai. One of them spelled เต่า as *dtào* and the other as *tao*. The sounds *d* and *t* have a lot in common. In *phonetics*, which is the study of speech sounds, they're called *stops*, because for a moment all the air stops coming out of your mouth. In Thai, there are different stops than the *d* and *t* that we find in English. Some of them sound something in between. So, for this book, I picked *dtào*, because in this book *D is for Turtle*, but *T is for Octopus*.

Sometimes there are even MORE challenges! As a team, we set out to confirm each of these words with native speakers. But even then, different speakers of the same language can have different ideas about what the correct transliteration should be. What is the best Romanization of the Hebrew word for *octopus*? Is it *tmanun* or *tamnun*? Reasonable people will disagree, and it could start an interesting discussion about how language changes, or about the difference between consonants and vowels. In some cases, different dialects of a language use different words. For example, in Northern Kurdish, the word for *fox* is *rovî*, but in Central Kurdish, it is *rêwî*. In cases like this, we used the word that we were able to confirm with a native speaker. For consistency, when more than one word from a language is included in the book, we followed the style of one source. For example, both Cherokee words are transliterated following the SIYO Cherokee Language Engine, which also provides pronunciation recordings for each word.

Finally, the names of the languages represented in this book are written in English as they are commonly translated. For example, we use *French* instead of *Français*. These languages are currently spoken by a range of more than a billion speakers to a few hundred, and the 69 languages represented in this book are only a fraction of the more than 6,500 spoken across the world.

With gratitude to the Levine Querido team: Arthur Levine,
Meghan McCullough, Madelyn McZeal, Irene Vázquez, Nick Thomas, and
Antonio Gonzalez Cerna, and Andrea Wollitz at Recorded Books
for their enormous help in reaching out and connecting with friends, new
and old, who are native speakers of all these languages. And many thanks to
the speakers who shared their voices, words, and explanations. I learned
so much and wasn't even trying to translate a complete sentence!
Thank you.